FAMILY VALUES

From A-Z

JU'MOND NORMAN

AuthorHouse™
1663 Liberty Drive
Bloomington, IN 47403
www.authorhouse.com
Phone: 1 (800) 839–8640

Published by AuthorHouse 11/28/2018

ISBN: 978–1–5462–7042–3 (sc)
ISBN: 978–1–5462–7043–0 (e)

Library of Congress Control Number: 2018914122

Print information available on the last page.

This book is printed on acid–free paper.

authorHOUSE®

This book is dedicated to all parents (adopted parent, single parent, step-parents) everywhere, a child's most valuable teachers.

All of your family is
very important.

Brothers are very
helpful an kind.

Cats can be considered
family also.

Dogs are family
friends fore sure.

Every time I see family
I have lots of fun and I
learn more about them.

Family and Friends
are the people that
loves you the most.

Great things are achieved
when family works together.

Helping one another is
a true family value.

I try to be the best family
member I can be.

Just try to learn your family's
culture and history.

Know that family will
always love you.

Love and respect
family at all times.

My family all have
similar features.

New family members
are born every year.

Older family love story time.

I love both parts of my
family the same.

It's good to ask
questions about you.

Respect is a big part of family.

I always feel safe
around family.

Family time is the
best time of day.

Family will help you
get over and under all
of your problems.

I always value my
family's advice.

We are all family one
way or another.

Family is extremely
supportive of each other.

I'm the youngest
child in my family.

Family is always a safe zone.

My family is filled with love.

Printed in the United States
By Bookmasters